Fifteen to Infinity

to Allen,
with friendship + esteem,
from Ruth.

—

April 1984

[signature]

Fifteen to Infinity

Ruth Fainlight

Ruth Fainlight [signature]

Hutchinson

London Melbourne Sydney Auckland Johannesburg

Hutchinson & Co. (Publishers) Ltd

An imprint of the Hutchinson Publishing Group

17–21 Conway Street, London W1P 6JD

Hutchinson Group (Australia) Pty Ltd
30–32 Cremorne Street, Richmond South, Victoria 3121
PO Box 151, Broadway, New South Wales 2007

Hutchinson Group (NZ) Ltd
32–34 View Road, PO Box 40–086, Glenfield, Auckland 10

Hutchinson Group (SA) Pty Ltd
PO Box 337, Bergvlei 2012, South Africa

First published 1983
© Ruth Fainlight 1983

Set in VIP Bembo by
D. P. Media Limited, Hitchin, Hertfordshire

Printed in Great Britain by The Anchor Press Ltd
and bound by Wm Brendon & Sons Ltd,
both of Tiptree, Essex

British Library Cataloguing in Publication Data
Fainlight, Ruth
  Fifteen to infinity
  I. Title
  821'.914   PR6056.F/

ISBN 0 09 152471 7

In memory of my mother

ACKNOWLEDGEMENTS

Ambit
Critical Quarterly
Descant
English
European Judaism
The Fiction Magazine
Grand Street
Here Now
The Hudson Review
The Jewish Chronicle
The Jewish Quarterly
The Literary Review
The London Magazine
The London Review of Books
New Letters
New Statesman
Only Poetry
Outposts
Pacific Quarterly Moana
Poems for Shakespeare no. 9
Poetry (Chicago) CXLI No. 6 – for *Passions* and *The Prism*
Quarto
Siting Fires
The Threepenny Review
Times Literary Supplement

Contents

I

Passenger

Not watching trains pass and dreaming of when
I would become that traveller, glimpsed
inside the carriage flashing past a watching
dreaming child, but being the passenger

staring out at tall apartment blocks
whose stark forms cut against the setting sun
and bars of livid cloud: balconies crowded
with ladders, boxes, washing, dead pot-plants,

into lighted, steamy windows where women
are cooking and men just home from work, shoes
kicked off and sleeves rolled up, are smoking, stretched
exhausted in their sagging, half-bought chairs,

under viaducts where children busy
with private games and errands wheel and call
like birds at dusk: all that urban glamour
of anonymity which makes me suffer

such nostalgia for a life rejected
and denied, makes me want to leave the train,
walk down the street back to my neighbourhood
of launderettes, newsagents, grocery shops,

become again that watching dreaming girl
and this time live it out – one moment only
was enough before a yawning tunnel-
mouth obscured us both, left her behind.

Here

Here, like a rebel queen
exiled to the borderlands,
the only role I can assume
is Patience, the only gesture,
to fold my hands and smooth
my robe, to be the seemly one,

the only precept, always
to know the truth, even if forced
to silence, never to deny
my unrepentant nature.
I am my own tamer.
This life is the instrument.

And yet the iron hand wears
such a velvet glove,
and dreams and memories
of prelapsarian happiness –
simple actions which, when
first performed, lacked that content –

return to slow my steps
as I climb up and down between
the parlour and the kitchen
to fill my watering-can again
and give the plants their ration,
makes me question that self-image.

Some power, created by
an altered vision, moving
to a different rhythm,
annihilates the past, revealing
space enough for another
universe. And there,

where needs and wishes synchronize,
where truth is changed and laws
revised, the capital has fallen
to a friendly tribe,
and I can leave this exile
when I choose, or rule from here.

Stubborn

My Stone-Age self still scorns
attempts to prove us more
than upright animals
whose powerful skeletons
and sinewy muscled limbs
were made to be exhausted
by decades of labour
not subdued by thought,

despises still those dreamers
who forget, poets
who ignore, heroes
who defy mortality
while risking every failure,
spirits unsatisfied
by merely their own
bodily survival.

I know her awful strength.
I know how panic, envy,
self-defence, are mixed
with her tormented rage
because they will deny
her argument that nothing
but the body's pleasure,
use, and comfort, matters.

Guarding her cave and fire
and implements, stubborn
in her ignorance,
deaf to all refutation,
I know she must insist
until the hour of death
she cannot feel the pain
that shapes and haunts me.

Outside the Mansion

As though we stood with noses pressed against the glass
of a window-pane, outside a mansion, dazzled by
the glowing lamps, the music and the circling dancers:

festivity, ceremony, celebration –
all equally alien to my sort of person.
Such a failing passes down the generations.

It could well be a fairy story, half-remembered.
I often wonder if some godmother uninvited
to the party, vengeful, cast her mournful spell.

So profoundly known, the joyless spite spoilers
use to ease self-inflicted pain; envy
and disappointment proudly claim choice of the poison

they gag and choke on. Growing older, closer
to my sources, I almost understand now why
the warmest most confiding moment must provoke

a cursed inherent disavowal and contempt
of every garland placed to decorate that brow
and hide those eyes before whose gaze we're powerless.

Stronger than the doubt of being right or wrong,
that refusal is our one tradition. We watch
the windows darken as the curtains slide across.

The Prism

Braided like those plaits of multi–
coloured threads my mother kept
in her workbox (beige, flesh, and fawn
for mending stockings, primary tones
to match our playclothes, grey and black
for Daddy's business suits), or Medusa-
coils of telephone wires, vivid
as internal organs exposed in their packed
logic under the pavement, nestling
in the gritty London clay,
associations fray into messages:

codes to unravel, cords to follow
out of prison, poems which make
no concession, but magnify
the truth of every note and colour,
indifferent whether they blind or deafen
or ravish or are ignored; the blueprint
of a shelter against the glare
– and the waterfall to build it near –
the perfect place to sit and hear
that choir of hymning voices, and watch
the prism of the rainbow spray.

Entries

Like notes of music black against the stave,
the look of words and letters in purposeful
groupings, whether printed or written, seems
to convey something more definite than
their overt message, even when understood.

But, thorns on the knotted stems of briars
thick as the hundred-year growth around the sleeping
princess, or a spider-web's decoration

15

(dried-up flies like November blackberries,
legs contracted in death), how well they hide it.

Dark beetles, swimmers with glistening backs,
etching their hieroglyphs between worm-casts and
    pebbles;
bird-claw cuneiform and rabbit-tracks
across dawn's snow-fall, runic silhouettes
of trees upon the sunset-streaked horizon,
the icicles' oghamic alphabet,

each mark, spoor, trace, or vestige left,
every shadow that stirs the wheatfield as if
a god strode there, are the imaginings
and melody of energies beyond
control until expressed: entries in
the dictionary of another language.

Observations of the Tower Block

During the day, the building becomes a gigantic machine
collecting data from the whole district. At night,
a Cunard liner with every cabin occupied,
rigging decorated for the final gala.

Different patterns of lights. No matter how late I go
to bed or early I wake, there are always lights burning.
Nights of insomnia, when I look out the window,
someone else in the building is also not sleeping.

The lights glow pink and yellow, green and orange.
Is it from coloured bulbs, or filtered through curtains?
Who are the people who live in those apartments?

Illuminated lift-shafts, halls, and balconies.
The grid of the structure determines these lives, but my
    sightings
are too irregular to grasp their pattern or meaning.

16

Author! Author!

What I am working at and want to perfect –
my project – is the story of myself: to have it
clear in my head, events consecutive,
to understand what happened and why it happened.

I wander through department-stores and parks,
beyond the local streets, seem to be doing
nothing; then an overheard phrase or the way light
slants from the clouds, unravels the hardest puzzle.

It takes so much time, uses all my energy.
How can I live, here and now, when the past
is being unwound from its great spindle, and tangles
forgotten motives around the present?

Rather than set the record straight, further
knowledge complicates. I cannot stop
the action to make a judgement, or hope for better.
Every gesture casts a longer shadow

into the future, each word shifts the balance.
I see myself as one more character
in this extravagant scenario,
the story not yet finished. And who's the author?

Sediments

The moment the door closed, your smile fell like cigar ash
onto the carpet, leaving as little trace,
and once again alone, off-guard, worn out
by the party you had to work so hard at –

all that's left to do now is rinse out
the glasses and raise the window to air the place,
watch the brake-lights interweave their pattern
up the boulevard and throw the butts out,
pull the heavy curtains to then undress
and slowly clean the makeup from your face
while your brain keeps circling round that print-out
of what you meant but never got to say,

until the bath filled with its scented comfort,
and afterwards (the naked footstep marked
so clearly in the talcum powder spilled out
across the floor is like a castaway's)
you take the silver pill-box from your handbag
and wide awake though tired enough to pass out,
lie down on the bed and feel the swirling
sediment dissolving in your veins.

Death's Love-Bite

A slow-motion explosion is what my mouth's become,
front teeth thrusting forward at impossible angles.
Incisors once in satisfactory alignment
cruelly slice through lips and tongue, and molars grind
each other into powder. Though it took almost thirty
years for them to drift so far apart, the pace
accelerates. My mouth contains meteors
and molecules, the splintered bones of mastodons,
galaxies and Magellanic clouds; feels like
a photograph of particles halted in
a cyclotron and magnified a thousand powers,
a microscopic re-enactment of the planet's
coming total fracture, elements dispersing
out in space. That's the truth I clench between
my jaws, behind my face. And all the technical
ingenuity called upon to solve
this dental problem won't heal Death's love-bite.

Silk Kimonos

Jade green and pale gold
under dark autumn cloud, worn flimsy
by rain and frost and wind, the plane's
leaves shift across their boughs
and the closed fronts of houses like silk
kimonos over dancers' limbs.

The Journey

Head against the glass, eyes close
to the train window, everything that grows
along the siding blurs and streaks: a green
and brown and yellow diagram of speed.

Not until I urge my gaze backwards
down the line can I distinguish saplings,
plumy grasses, flowering weeds and briars
sown there haphazard. Lifting my eyes higher,

one pigeon, pale against thunder-clouds,
spot-lit by a fitful summer sun,
rises above a formal wood, dense
trees all the same size, as though planted together.

Softened by the mirror of a tunnel,
my reflected face stared out, much younger,
superimposed like an old photograph.
If I sat opposite, one glance

comparing the two would be enough to inform
myself of every change that time has wrought.
Suddenly, I learned I was not other,
earlier, than what I have become

but only now am forced to recognize.
Wings beating it further up the sky,
from a bird's-eye view, the whole route is visible.
The nature of the country makes no difference,

nor the hastening traveller's confusion
(journey still unended, memories unproved)
between conflicting versions of the legend
which unites such images and questions

concerning destiny and chance. Dazzle
of sunlight, then shadow, blinding me in the carriage.
A horse alone in a meadow, the level-crossing.
A steeple. The first houses. The train is stopping.

Launching

Autumn. Early morning.
A bench near the pond in Kensington
Gardens. This park is where
I've watched the seasons change
for twenty years. Under
my feet, yellow and crimson
leaves, colours as pure
as though with death their poisons
were purged – but further away,
against an empty sky,
the rusty foliage
of a shrubbery like a head
of hennaed greying hair.

Through the playground railings
the swings and slide and sandbox
I feared and hated. No one
told me how short such moments
were, nor taught the art
of living in the present.

There seemed so many dream-
scenarios. Now,
the only roles left: leathery
tourist, plastic-bag crazy,
reclusive autodidact, or
admirer of grandchildrens'
model racing yachts.

Spring and summer passed,
winter marking its own
bright blaze on what will not
endure, the balance shifts
from hope to human nature,
and the last self manifests,
poised for survival. But meanwhile
come days like this, when nothing
yet seems crucial, blue
and gold and calm, with time
to feed the ducks and learn
the different styles of launching
boats into the water.

After Fifteen
to David

First there were close-ups: fallen petals,
patterned bark, fungus on stones,
a baby's pram – garden scenes.
The playground where, laughing and rosy-
cheeked, you waddled after pigeons
in your padded snow-suit; I,
another discontented mother
by the sandbox. All photographs
which seemed to need between three and six
feet. Then the focus shifted,
lengthened, changed. Now, Sunday
morning in the park, six feet
tall, you stand against the peeling

plane-trunk, look up through its leafless
twigs and branches, camera aimed
at pallid winter clouds. 'Fifteen
to infinity?' you ask, to confirm
the setting. Yes. You have grown
to become the photographer, and time
expands around you like the dizzying
crown of the tree and sky above:
fifteen to infinity.

Love-Feast

Sulphur-yellow mushrooms like unlaid, unshelled eggs
inside a chicken's stomach when my mother cleaned it.
This morning, mushrooms on the lawn made me
    remember.

Bright as dew on the grass and silver with air-bubbles,
a stream of water splashed from the dull brass tap against
the side of the sink and over her red-chilled fingers when she
opened the carcase and laughed to show me how some
    were almost
ready – yolks only needing their coating of lime and mucus,
while others were still half-formed, small as pearls or seeds.

Always, once the chicken was plucked and quartered and
    boiling,
my mother would take those eggs, marked with twisting coils
of crimson threads like bloodshot eyes, and the liver put aside
on the draining-board in a chipped old china saucer, and
    fry them
with an onion to make our private treat. In the steamy
kitchen, the two of us would eat, and love each other.

Handbag

My mother's old leather handbag,
crowded with letters she carried
all through the war. The smell
of my mother's handbag: mints
and lipstick and Coty powder.
The look of those letters, softened
and worn at the edges, opened,
read, and refolded so often.
Letters from my father. Odour
of leather and powder, which ever
since then has meant womanliness,
and love, and anguish, and war.

War-Time

'Stand here in front of me,' my mother said,
and pushed me forward in the downtown office
doorway. 'Hide me.' Behind my back, she fumbled
with a sagging stocking and broken garter.

That garter: salmon-pink elastic crinkled
at the edges, half-perished, stretched too often,
it had lost the rubber button. Her stockings were
always too long. Something else to blame her for.

Turning quickly, I was shocked to see
the folded rayon top expose an inch
or two of thigh – soft white flesh, neglected,
puckered with cold. (Yet another torment.)

Her round felt hat, pierced by a tarnished arrow
glinting in the drafty corner, bent lower
than my ten-year-old shoulder, and the safety-pin
held between her lips seemed further off

than that umbrella-tip or those galoshes
of distracted passers. For nobody noticed
or cared but me – the judging daughter, who had made
herself the substitute for an absent father.

Her flushed face. My harsh stern eye. My impulse
to hurt and to love, towards and away. That rainy
winter day, my mother and I determined
a future no peace-time knowledge can assuage.

Or Her Soft Breast

I could not get to sleep last night,
burning on the slow fire
of self-despite,

twisting on the spit that's thrust and
turned in such cruel manner
by my own hand,

until those earthy clinging arms
lifted out of the dark
to hold me fast

and drag me back to the same place
I thought I had escaped,
to see her face

as close as when I knew it first:
smiling, tender, perfect.
My fetters burst,

but the puzzle and the meaning
of my sudden freedom –
her touch on me,

soothing and cool, as though I sank
into a pool and drank
there, thankful –

was it a dream of love or death?
The grave, where I now slept,
or her soft breast?

Lost Drawing

Bare winter trees in silhouette
against a clear cold turquoise sky
just after sunset: during the war,
at my aunt's house in Virginia, I tried
to draw them – trees like these in England
which she never saw – and now,
trees in my garden make me feel
the first true pang of grief since her death.

Between the wash-tubs and storecupboards filled
with pickled peaches and grape jam, crouched
into a broken wicker chair,
I peered up through the basement window.
Sketchpad on my lap, with brushes and
bottles of black ink, blue ink, and water,
I wanted to convey the thickness
of their trunks, the mystery
of how a branch puts out a hundred
twigs, the depth and power of evening.

I heard her cross the porch, the kitchen
floorboards creak. As it grew darker,
that halo of light, outlining
all the finest intersections,
faded. Night absorbed the trees
the house the woman and the girl
into itself, kept every aspect
of that time alive, to give
me back today the memory
of my dead aunt and my lost drawing.

25

Crystal Pleating
for A.G.

Crystal pleating around the neck and shoulders
of that flamboyant crêpe dress I only wore once –
I remember the two of us shopping for it. Since then,
pushed into the back of the wardrobe, covered
with a dusty plastic, I've watched it fade
the way black dyestuffs do, to grey and copper-
purple, except those jetty streaks in folds
and hem. If mine now seems a witch's costume,
the queenly robe of silver-white you chose
must be all tarnished, should any part remain.
What a pair we looked. I knew how much
you needed me as a foil: the negative
of such a vivid presence. Love made me glad
to serve your purpose. But my regard was not
enough, nor what you wanted – and though the dress
would be quite perfect as a mourning-garment,
I have not dared to put it on again.

The Storm

Harry, I know how much you would have enjoyed it.
I can see your mouth's ironic curve as the heavens
opened. The umbrella over my head was almost
useless – rain and hail at the same slant
as your amused imagined gaze darkened
the side of my coat and trousers. Hard to resist
the thought that while we hurried back to the car
as soon as we could to wait it out, cold
and distracted, someone up there was paying attention,
taking notice. The sky had been clear

enough as we drove through the cemetery
gates into those horizontal acres
ignored behind the bonfire sites and toolsheds
of suburban gardens, then parked and walked
between memorial stones to our appointment.
A spare man in a mac held the casket
chest-high as he approached. I stretched
a finger to touch a corner. The brass plate,
engraved with your full name, flashed paler
in the altering light as clouds thickened.

Cut into the piece of ground that was
the grave of both our parents – a square hole,
its soil piled nearby. A superstitious
qualm made me look down: too shallow
to disturb them. It must have been the very
moment the sexton stooped to put your ashes
there – where I hoped you'd want to be:
with them – that the storm broke. Instead of a struggle
with grief, we were fighting the weather, reduced to
the ludicrous; instead of prayer, a dry
shelter was what seemed most important. Water
running across my hands, inside my sleeves,
I took the spade and being chief mourner,
made the first movement to bury you. Harry,
I think you would have found the symbolism
too facile and pompous, and your sense
of humour stopped you taking it seriously,
though certainly delighted by the conceit
of Nature aghast and weeping at your interment,
my poor brother, her true and faithful poet.

In Memoriam H.P.F.

God, the dead, and Dona Elvira
all inhabit the same realm:
the great democracy of Imagination.

Every paradise and underworld
beyond a blue horizon –
Sheol or Elysium –
is a beautiful product of mental function:
conjuration, prayer, and purpose.

I shall not meet my dead again
as I remember them
alive, except in dreams or poems.
Your death was the final proof
I needed to accept that knowledge.

II

As Though She were a Sister

As though she were an older or a younger
sister, whom I might bully, flout, ignore
or use, my dealings were not serious
enough. How could I think she was my sister?
What insolence – and luck, to dodge her well-
deserved rebuke. For she, more like a mother
(I the disrespectful child who shouts
and flails and pulls away) till now has not
abandoned or betrayed me. I must have seemed
ridiculous or worse to all who watched –
and most to those who recognized the Muse.

Spring in Ladbroke Square

Embers still coated with ash,
these February buds – while others
already show the glowing nub
of life, each one Dionysus'
cone-tipped staff; and the first raw leaves
unhusked seem frail red curds and fibres
of flesh clinging to the twigs, as though
bacchantes had been here last night
to carry out spring's sacrifice,
and thrown the torn and bloody shreds
of Orpheus' limbs into the branches.

Ulysses, Troilus, and Cressida

Each infidelity left Ulysses
more uneasy. (What was Penelope doing?)
He knew that every woman was a whore –
why else were they here? – while warriors
were enemies only when they fought.

A guest in Menelaus' camp, that boy,
Troilus, brother of Hector (what joy to meet him
on the battlefield!) was being fooled.
It made him furious. His first look
at Cressida enough to guess the truth:
a daughter of the game. No doubt about
his duty. In spite of worldly wisdom, talk
of enterprise and reason, on one well-worn
subject Thersites was no fouler. She
personified expediency: a born
survivor – he understood and loathed the type.

It's called a tragedy, though none of these three
dies. And yet if every change brings death
nearer, to tear the scales from Troilus' eyes
was murder; while Cressida resigned herself
to the fortunes of war, and Ulysses sailed home.

Marvellous Toys

*(with acknowledgements to Marcel Detienne
& Jean Pierre Vernant)*

How was Dionysus captured by the Titans?
With marvellous toys: a cone, emblem of
the goddess; a pierced stone that roared like a bull;
a tuft of wool, like those his killers used
to daub on gypsum and disguise themselves;

a knucklebone, which grants divinatory
powers; golden apples as his passport
to Elysium; and a round mirror
to see his ghostly other image – what child,
no matter how divine, could ever resist?

Who wanted Dionysus' death? Hera,
furious, had plotted to destroy him
in Semele's womb. Her malign advice
ignored, next she goaded Zeus to launch
a thunderbolt against the moony girl –

but the six-month child was sewn into his father's
thigh, for when the time arrived he must
be born. Yet wherever the boy was kept,
Hera's vengeful eyes pierced his disguise.
She sent her hit-men, the seven simple Titans.

What did the murderers do to Dionysus?
They cut his body into seven parts
which first they boiled and then they barbecued
(reversing ritual procedure), but the heart
was put aside, to be saved by Athene his sister.

Why did Dionysus triumph? From
his beating heart, the vital central organ,
he was resurrected to defeat the Titans
(whose blood and ashes formed the human race)
and open the cycle of death and generation;

and horned like a goat or stag or ram, raging
over the mountains with his pack of Maenads and Satyrs
brandishing cone-tipped ivy-twined spears and tearing
apart whatever they met – to bring drunkenness
and madness: those marvellous toys of paradise.

Death of Adonis

The Muses, daughters of Memory,
avenged themselves on Aphrodite
for being forced to couple with mortals
and bear their progeny; the weapon
was a magic hunting song.
The haunting lyric lured Adonis,
her sweet lover, so unwarrior-
like, toward that fatal meeting
in the forest where, under
a mast-oak, his unhappy rival
Ares waited, transformed by jealous
rage into a boar. And even

as her darling's life-blood poured
away and stained the anemones,
to prove Art's power over Love's,
the Mountain Muses soothed the weeping
goddess with another story.

Titian's 'Venus and Adonis'

He with that calculating look,
sated, half-rueful, of the local heart-breaker –
mustachioed garage-mechanic – and she,
the blacksmith's wife from further down
the square, mortified yet pleading:
why should he want to leave all
that lavish flesh and golden hair?

Even Cupid is asleep, drugged
by her perfume and odours, his quiver of arrows
abandoned – but the dogs turn back to their master
and pull at their leashes, as though they sniffed
the waiting boar, and the plume in Adonis's
jaunty cap, stirred by the autumn
wind (perfect hunting weather,
sun pouring through thunder-clouds)
is equally restless. Nothing will thwart him.
Her insistence seems futile, his young
arrogance triumphant, and yet,
her power has never failed before.

Susannah and the Elders

Sometimes she's painted clothed, but most
prefer her naked; she's shown at various
ages: a sturdy angry girl
able to fight back – then more
submissive: flesh to eye and handle
by merchants choosing cattle, or ancients
hoping to regain their youth.

Often the elders are timid, crouch
under balustrades, hide in the bushes,
peer around statuary. But when the maidservants
leave her alone in the garden, bolder
and lecherous, the turbanned, scrawny-necked fools
creep to the foreground, pluck at her towels
and drapery, encourage each other with grimaces.

Yet no matter how passive she seems: complacent,
frightened, or even peacefully unaware
of their presence, always she inhabits
a separate universe, realm
of the indifferent good; purified
with living waters, become
a talisman of flesh and blood.

The Noonday Devil

Demon of accidie, the noonday devil.
How well I know his power – he, who besieges
the soul, slackens the hands and will, holds the sun
still, and makes each hour as long as fifty.

A bowl of lukewarm milk where flies settle:
my mind, subjected to these restless thoughts,
this weary languor – until I hate my work,
my room, my friends, myself, and my ambitions.

Under his torpid spell my life seems endless:
fallow earth and unused, rusty plough;
a waterless cloud that never lets down rain;
a tree too often transplanted whose roots have withered.

Some days I can muster all my strength
for combat; others, just endure his torments.
But I have lost my hope in prayers and tears,
my appetite for anguish. Sloth always wins.

The Song of Matho-Talen
(the last voluntary victim)

Like priestesses in megalithic
times, ancient village mothers
still Death's celebrants and agents

take the consecrated hammer
from Carnac chapel from Morbihan
and raise it in your freckled hands

to crack my skull release me from
life's burden and death's terror,
in honour of the trinity you serve

be kind as to your favoured youngest
son or each dead Pope whose head
is tapped three times with a silver mallet

then lay me near the seven sleepers'
stone to let my spirit turn
the wind and bring good fishing weather.

Miriam's Well
(from Talmudic sources)

On Sabbath evening, Miriam's Well,
and all its healing miracles –
that holy liquid which for her sake
saved the children of Israel, followed
them through the desert forty years –
moves from well to river, from river
to stream to well.
                     After her death,
the flowing rock of Miriam's Well
sank in the sea, to rise again each
Sabbath and work its wonders. Miriam
died by a kiss from God. The Angel

of Death could not take her, nor worms
touch her body. When you draw the bucket
from Miriam's Well, if you want to hear
her prophesy, remember to fill
your mouth with water.

The Mount of Olives

Eternity has staked its claim
to the hills around Jerusalem.
The dead have prime territory,
every slope a cemetery,
caves, crypts, and sepulchres,
catacombs hollowed out like ovens
under olive groves and churches.

Cars and buses grind their way
below the Walls and up the valley.
Today, you are the only ones
who want to have the door into
the Sanctuary of Ascension
opened, the boy there told us. How
can I make a living without tourists?

Sitting on a rock beside
the Tomb of the Prophets, two men,
deaf and dumb, talk with their hands.
If across the Kidron Brook
the Golden Gate unlocked to let
Messiah through and the resurrected
sang his praises, would they notice?

But still the dead ones sleep like babies
undisturbed by bombs, while above them –
rosy as cooks, stern as Crusaders,
pale as Hassids, watchful as soldiers,
silent as angels – spirits hover,
and Eternity settles deeper into
the land around Jerusalem.

That Sinaitic Landscape –

where the sky divides
into separate zones
with hostile atmospheres
rules and powers
white over earth
pale as clinkered ash
blue over ocean

the change defined
by shoreline groves of palms
a sudden glimpse
of dark-skinned nomads
and under its glittering skin
even the sea looks softer
than this astringent desert

where bullet-holed tanks
abandoned shell-casings
rust-ruined scorch-marked
transport carriages
and twisted railway lines

guns with their barrels spiked
curling back like petals
of parched gigantic flowers
or animals trapped in crusted
opalescent salt-pans
braying out their thirst
all appear like some
elaborate mirage

remembered now in winter
in a peaceful city
image of a world
distant as a star
close as war.

(1979)

Archive Film Material

At first it seemed a swaying field of flowers
windblown beside a railway track, but then
I saw it was the turning heads of men
unloaded from the cattle trucks at Auschwitz.

At the Basilica

Spattered like bloody drops across the broken marble
    floor
at the Basilica, a molten spoor

of coins fused verdigris by centuries into the stone:
Alaric's plundering hordes. The sack of Rome.

Leonard Baskin's Death Drawings

I. Death the Gladiator

He looks like the oldest gladiator left,
the only survivor from seasons of murderous games;
a pensioned-off mercenary from the border
campaigns, veteran of every atrocity.

Under the arena – those passageways
as complicated as the convolutions
of a brain exposed by primitive trepanning,
that warren of storerooms and cellars where animals
and slaves, weapons and chariots, are kept,
venue for perverse experiments,
their walls of kidney-coloured brick rotten
with sweat of fear and pain – lies his kingdom:
trainer of the Colosseum's favourites.

II. Death's Labour

Sated and exhausted Death,
head bent forward, heavy skull
a universe of unredeemable
flesh, scabbed bald cranium
a schoolroom globe marked with only
the largest seas and continents.

Sagging dugs, bursting thighs,
belly like a pregnancy
(womb to hold an ogre's foetus),
gross and epicene, he's glutted,
stupefied. Sick from over-
eating that eternal harvest

of corpses, he gags and vomits; gorged
beyond endurance, lowers himself
back as though onto a close-stool.

Eyes sunk deep in their sockets (candles
guttering out, choked by matter)
teeth worn down by endless grinding
of bones, nose corroded like an old
syphilitic's. But lax across
one knee, the bruised meaty hand
of a labourer. Death works hard.

III. Death's Cloak

His fuscous wings could be a cloak,
its ruffled feathers, incrustations
on an insect's carapace,

the chrysallis that broke to show
his arrogant incarnation –
his evil glutted baby face

his massive and hairless torso –
the god whose cruel dilaceration,
limb from limb, of all the human race

no one escapes, as though for sport
he thus torments, exterminates,
and we the writhing worms impaled

upon his stabbing beak, or summer
insects in his vigorous hands.

IV. Death with no Wings

It is the death you saw –
the hands of a Japanese wrestler
reaching out for you, tendons tense
and stretched, the brutal forearms
of a weightlifter, a prizefighter,
a porter from the meat market.

Nostrils like nares in a skull,
mouth a wound's torn lips,
tiny ears and eyes, head sunk
between the slab-slopes of his shoulders,
no neck. Great belly
and heraldic genitals.
Flesh pink-raw and hairless.

It is the death that comes with no pity
to thrust you into the charnel-pit.
Death with no wings.

V. This Meat

This meat browning for our meal –
these charred woody fibres where
the seared surface seals and darkens,
clings to the pan, is what must have stuck
to the bars of St Lawrence's grille or
the iron beds of Phnom Pen. The sound
flesh gave as the heat took was unheard
then through cries of pain. Here
in my kitchen I am forced to look and listen.
I cannot ignore it. This meat
is the same stuff I am made from. This
meat I cook now for our meal.

III

Trompe L'Oeil
(at the Villa Farnesina)

A blank niche in a wall
that you walk towards
with a vase in your hand
to place on the painted pedestal.
The pieces of broken glass
the bent stems
and fallen petals
and on the floor a pool of water –
yourself putting them there.

Red Message

Stern ancestors, with faces as intricate
as Japanese print-makers' seals or circuits
of transistor-cells. Wherever you lived,
flesh and bone of the clan became that place,
lives gone into the earth like water
poured for ritual, or dark ash strewn
from a sacrifice. Programmed by return
and repetition, watching the changing pattern
of smoke and sparks and leaves made time
another code to break – a white cataract
crashing over the head, or flames transmitting
their red message from the funeral pyre.

Spring Light

These first few days after the clocks change
and darkness comes an hour later
(the start of Summer Time)

seem to hurt most, deal the cruellest blow.
The weather gets colder. Winter won't go,
puts up one last fight.

Though sunshine at an unfamiliar angle
through the window shows a haggard
face with harsh new lines,

and restless during lengthened afternoons
you're forced to realize how soon
the reckoning arrives.

Every year, spring's return brings
it nearer, marks it clearer with
that unrelenting light.

Not Yet Enough

Spring: this shadow following
my hand and pen across the paper
after months of greyness. This shrinking
from the warmth upon my face
and shoulder, as though cold winter held me
pressed against my will to wear
its armour, and neither mid-day's altered
zenith, nor flowers' triumph, have power,
heat, or colour yet enough
to let me cast my shield and helmet
off, lay sword and dagger by,
and plunge into the garden's glare.

Spring in the City

Petals from the trees
along the street
revolve and fall.
Complex currents
lift them up toward
the boughs from which
their flight was launched.

All the space between
the rows of houses
in swirling movement
like sand in a rock-pool
as the sea sluices through
raising fine clouds
that blur its clearness.

Gutters choked with blossom
pavements patterned
the wind-blown hair of girls
tangled with blossom
a swarm of insects
aquarium of fishes
snowflakes in a storm.

Shaken by the breeze
and cornering cars
reaffirming the spiral
of the galaxies
the air today seems thick
with stardust and we
are breathing stars.

The Power Source

In this part of the country
all through July, sometimes
round the clock, after
the first crop's cut and stacked,
the rape-seed brought inside
that new blue corrugated
plastic barn behind
the churchyard, the driers keep blowing.
Industrial farming. Often
annoying, ignored, it fades into
the background: one more factor
in the ambient pattern of sound.

I can let it lower my guard
and mood – becoming sulky,
agitated – or get me
high on the idea of progress:
a theme to brood on. Either
way, stimulated or
nerve-wracked, I find the summer
different than before
I noticed the strain of trying
to be a nature-poet
these unbucolic days.
The power source has shifted.

When it stops, though other
motors seem much louder:
passing tourist traffic,
helicopters spraying,
tractors (drivers earphoned
to muffle their own noise),
the vital note is missing.
I wait its starting-up,
knowing I'll be uneasy
in the interval
between now and the August
combine-harvesters.

The Angel

Sometimes the boulder is rolled away,
but I cannot move it when
I want to. An angel must. Shall
I ever see the angel's face,
or will there always only be
that molten glow outlining every
separate hair and feathered quill,
the sudden wind and odour, sunlight,
music, the pain of my bruised shoulders.

The Concept

How it chills, that formulated
strategy toward a planned
objective, as though events must follow
an ordered sequence: the well–thought–out
campaign of progress from glacis to rampart

almost by the clock (glancing
over the other's nearer shoulder
at a wristwatch, the only accoutrement left
on a body that should be entirely naked)
calling up the memories
of times I was the possible conquest,

the concept of seduction marked the one
who, still in thrall to all
the old manoeuvres, could not dare
enough to let whatever happens
happen: such as making love.

Valleys and Mountains

What I know are valleys
between the mountains
have buried beneath them
the crests of other mountains,

and I can see through depths
of stormy ocean
the drowned empires
there before the ocean,

trace the cool fern's pattern
in burning coal,
ancient sunlit
jungles become black coal,

and proving every tale
concerning love's
transforming power –
surely this must be love.

Natural History

– then you captured my distracted spirit
and brought it down from where it danced and hovered
around our heads, brought me back to myself
trammelled by your gross and loving grasp,
into the realm of our own natural history,

into that garden where the flowers strain
on bristling stems toward the sun and arch
their petals wider, and the snail's slime-trail
stops at a broken shell as the harsh triumphant
beak stabs over and over through its pulpy heart,

where sounds and smells and colours, taste and touch
of hair and flesh, glistenings, swollen
heats and tension, matter's prodigal
and irresistible excess, all
transform the butterfly into a rutting primate.

Passions

Let's not mention love. It's like a glowing
stove to someone covered with burns already.
And hate is that dark cave whose depths conceal
a reeking oubliette where rivals groan.
One glimpse enough to turn your head
and make you lose your balance, envy will have
you spiralling from the top of the cliff, down
onto the breakers. Anger is the sea.
Gasping and buffeted, no matter how
you struggle or plead for mercy, you drown. But pride
can clothe those shattered bones with perfect skin,
and breathe into the lover's mouth her song.

The Music

I sit alone in my room
on a cold summer afternoon
upstairs from where you in your room
are playing the gramophone.
Though you don't know it, I open
my own door wide enough
to share the sound of the music.

Another floor up, in the attic,
two adolescent lovers
play a childhood game, just
rediscovered. Laughs, and the rattle
of dice, drift down from above.

Barely more than their age,
hidden on the steps below
the next-door villa, whose stones
still held the heat of day,
my head on your shoulder,
we listened to someone
playing the same tune.

That night, we hurried home
to our new games – perhaps
your memories are the same?
Or else, I have to wonder
why you chose the music.

Calcutta

Carts loaded with sacks and planks
moving into the pre-dawn city.
One man in front between the shafts,
two pushing from the back.

Knees drawn up to the chin,
rickshaw-men asleep
on the poles of their vehicles –
black crows roosting.

A five a.m. sweeper,
stiff-legged, stooping
at an empty crossing
by the silent kiosks.

The gaunt fronts of hospitals,
their windows bright
as strings of coloured lights cascading
down this wedding pavilion.

And now the hired car goes past
another drug-store, another clinic,
the Panacea Laboratory,
another sweet-shop.

Dark brick obelisks and pyramids
along the ruined paths –
'. . . . guide on young men,
the bark that's freighted with your country's doom':

Derozio's memorial –
and Rose Aylmer dead
in the Park Street cemetery.
Blood and marigolds at the Kalighat.

Give that girl thirty pice
because she's singing.
But don't look at the lepers'
blunted fingers.

In the Tibetan Restaurant, drinking gin,
middle-class intellectuals
to whom the greatest insult
is to be accused of pity,

and out at Dum Dum airport,
rising above the burning cow-dung pall
that blurs the skyline, another tourist
who can't take any more.

Birds in India

A crow cawing, and I remember
pale Calcutta mornings, sky
nacreous with pollution. A pigeon
burbling, I recall the look
of blurred mountains pushing up
through putty-coloured land within
the moving circle of the plane's
horizon, sandy water-courses
looped and plaited round Orissan
villages, paddy fields
and tracts of swampy ground the same
vivid green as parrots' wings –
there were so many resting on
the casuarina trees, beneath
the domes and arches of the Lodi
tombs near my hotel at Delhi.

The sound of birds now doesn't make
me think of English country gardens
or a London park. A month
of travelling was enough to alter
the associations, infect me
with this nostalgia for
storks seen from the train or peacocks
by a bathing tank or even
vultures flapping in a ditch
along the road to Udaipur.
It's not to watch the birds or be an
amateur ornithologist
that I want to return.
The birds must signify the first
time I truly understood it:
another realm and dimension of life.

The Venetian Mask

Why did I buy a mask without a mouth?
A mute is no muse for a poet. Where was my guardian
angel when I chose? But I was drawn
to that gilded face, mournful muffled and closed
upon itself, as though petrified by Medusa.

I hang it on the wall of my room, a subject
for contemplation: the countenance of a poet
subdued; a warning example whose silent message
is more than loud enough to harden my
refusal of such investiture and doom.

Among a Thousand Others

All my material used up.
I have cannibalized myself
thoroughly. Or was it a thousand
others who consumed me?

If I had been able to decide
there would have been no material:
that was the prime dilemma
(among a thousand others).

However, though the flesh has gone
I still can make this skeleton
obey my orders: attrition's
instrument become

cruel as a shipwreck survivor –
marrowbones split and sucked
for more material:
a thousand other triumphs.

Products of the Pig

Once upon a time and long ago,
when I lived in Majorca,
they fattened pigs with over-ripe figs
before their slaughter. (They were delicious.)
This autumn, visiting
a London garden, I saw a fig tree,
branches leaden, leaves already fallen,
with small hard withered green fruits
that never had enough sun to ripen
stuck against the naked twigs:
like scabs, I thought at first, or little
pig-snouts. But then somehow they looked
so harmless – and jaunty –
surviving in England.

Acrobatic Full Moon

A fat but agile acrobat
from a Chinese circus, the moon contracts
and elongates, then flattens out
again, playing tricks with the clouds.
Or is it more a double-jointed
golden cat glimpsed between
gloomy jungle ferns, an orange
segment, an apricot-coloured egg
yolk slithering across the oily
surface of a frying pan?

Watching it pretend to be
a car's headlamp, the smiling face
of a Michelin-man, cloth-cap worn
at a rakish angle, I almost thought
a flowerpot of geraniums
nodding their heads in the pre-dawn wind
further down the empty street

was someone else still awake
leaning out to contemplate
the antic moon's variations.

Now at five o'clock this morning
standing in the same corner
to brew myself a cup of maté
where every evening, cooking dinner,
I look westward through the window
toward the sunset, I can see
the full moon slide below the trees
and blocks of flats, to vanish as
the room lights up behind my back –
heralding the next act.

Justice
(for Julia)

Hearing how a splendid girl argued
from London to Crewe with people who would not move
from seats she'd booked for a group of students; how,
determined they should not rest while her school-party
stood in the corridor – and after the guard
refused to help – she got down from the train
and found a policeman (on duty there because of
the football crowd) who followed her back to the
    carriage
and put them all into their rightful places,

rueful, I wondered whether memories
of being just as valiant and heroic
a champion of the oppressed, were true.
How honest are such anecdotes; was I
ever really naive or brave as that?
Now, I know, fear and rage would stop me
making more than the most formal protest,
and stifled anger seethe into a poison
that does not kill but only paralyses.

56

Was it merely youth: when not one problem
seemed beyond solution; and confident,
I knew that nothing less than total justice
for every person in the world – myself
and others equally – could be enough?
What happened then which left me banished
to this manoeuvre-ground of Good and Evil,
tormenting devils, and fallen angels whose fiery
swords bar me from the realm of justice.

Progress – an Incident

Two women on the train, holiday-makers,
discuss the likelihood of life 'out there'.
The older, uglier, and livelier,
who found the item in her paper which
inspires this conversation, is more excited.

'Maybe they'll help us,' she says, leaning forward,
spectacles reflecting sheep on the marshland,
the pale towers of a power station.
The other grudgingly becomes involved.
'We won't understand their language.' Rouged cheeks,
small shrewd eyes and arched nose, she's like
an Elizabethan portrait wearing crimplene
slacks and blouse from Marks and Spencer. Dowdier
in frock and cardigan, swollen-ankled
over slingback sandals, the enthusiast, uncertain
if she can convince, yet illumined by
an urgent vision, loudly states: 'It's progress.
Going to the planets.' 'They'll die before
they get there. What earthly good is that?' 'It won't be
in our time. It's for them who come after.' Suddenly
she looked down at her lap, and flushed beneath
that pragmatic, steady, doubting gaze.

The Circle

We did not meet that often: once
or twice a year for drinks, or walking
to the store we'd stop and talk –
she the village dowager
and I the foreigner who'd stayed
a while but then decamped, become
one of the weekend people. Always
I admired that upright stance
and gallant style, her undiminished
presence. She still could play the perfect
hostess: draw me out about
the house, the garden, and the children,
and not touch on the personal.

But the last time I saw her
(taking a short-cut through her orchard
to the river) she called me over,
inviting me to join her and the dogs.
I noticed she looked different.
Her eyes had never been so bright
before, nor cheeks so gaunt and flushed,
hair disordered, gestures bewildered.
I started to say the usual things
about the weather and crops when,
almost peremptorily, she
interrupted to ask: 'Tell me please,
do you enjoy fairy stories?'

It was the end of summer. I
remember apple-pickers watching
as we paced back and forth among
the trees and she described her pleasure
to re-discover those old tales;
and how I wanted to believe
that, like a circle closing, she
had made connection between past
and present. Months later, a bitter

April day, I hear the news.
The circle was a fairy-ring,
as false as fairy-gold, and nurses
guard her from a worse bewitchment.

Judgement at Marble Arch

Office-girls doing their lunch-time shopping.
Bewildered blond families up from the provinces.
Africans, Arabs, Italians and Spaniards,
cut-price tee-shirts, blue-jeans and haversacks,
oily exhaust-fumes and noisy rock-music –
hot August sunshine, then the first autumn shower.

Just past Lyons Corner House, near Marble Arch
underground station, I heard a low but penetrating
moan by my right shoulder, and turned to confront
a tangle of greying hair not quite concealing
eyes squeezed shut and open mouth (saliva stretched
in threads between the drawn-back lips) of a woman –
about my size and age – wailing her distress.
Her naked goatish legs in heavy shoes kept
stumbling forward, somehow avoiding all obstructions.
The large red plastic bag in her dirty hands
was held as though at any moment she
would cover her head to hide from the assault
of sound and sight, or use it to vomit in.

Someone else had noticed. A buxom matron.
Our doubtful glances intersected. Both of us
relieved from having to decide what to do – but wondering
whether, with the other as witness, we were now committed
to action, as well as pity and horror. Slowly,
through the midday throng, we followed after,
murmuring our uncertainty. Whenever

I got close enough to hear, she was still
mouthing her fear, and curses. The woman with me
seemed as nervous. 'I'm frightened,' I confessed.
'Me too.' The bright brown eyes of a good wife
and mother stared back, grateful for my frankness.

At Edgware Road a man reached out to touch her arm.
She had become visible. The circle of watchers
    broadened.
She flinched and dropped . . . then stretched the plastic
    bag
across her face as though it were a magic hood,
the fluttering red wings of a wounded bird,
a shaman's regalia with its tawdry glamour.
'Where's a policeman?' my companion muttered.
I had to get away. 'I'll try to find one.'

In another story I'd take her home and nurse her –
heal her, be a holy martyr – but I didn't
want to; nor did I want to hand her over.
When I returned from where I'd stood around the
    corner
in the hotel entrance, the crowd had scattered.
'She crossed the road,' the stranger said – alarmed,
perplexed, almost indignant. 'I thought there'd be
an accident.' 'Maybe she's been like this for years,'
I mumbled, ashamed of myself. 'So many sick people
in the cities . . . .' 'Perhaps.' For the first time
we had to deal with each other (if we talked longer
might be forced to make a judgement) so said goodbye,
and went back to our interrupted errands.

The Barrier

Up ahead, a tangle of rocks and earth
and caught twigs half damming a river
of rapid water under heavy branches.

The flow is almost halted: that steady movement
which unimpeded scoured the stream-bed deeper
and polished every stone, now baulked, reverses.

Behind the barrier, the new pool
slowly fills with dead fish and leaves.
The simpler life-forms take possession. Will

the next storm wash it clear, the stream run smooth
and vivid from its source; will the current
turn and broaden into a harbour?

The Future

The future is timid and wayward
and wants to be courted, will not
respond to threats or coaxing,
and hears excuses only
when she feels secure.

Doubt, uproar, jeers,
vengeful faces roughened
by angry tears, the harsh
odours of self-importance,
are what alarm her most.

Nothing you do will lure her
from the corner where
she waits like a nun of a closed
order or a gifted young
dancer, altogether

the creature of her vocation,
with those limits and strengths.
Trying to reassure her,
find new alibis
and organize the proof

of your enthralment and
devotion, seems totally useless –
though it teaches how
to calm your spirit, move
beyond the problem's overt

cause and one solution –
until the future, soothed now,
starts to plot another
outcome to the story:
your difficult reward.